BLESSED WITH TWO LIVES

A Story of Addiction, Recovery, and Redemption

HARRY JOHN OVEREND

ISBN: 978-1-4834-5568-6 (sc)
ISBN: 978-1-4834-5569-3 (e)

Library of Congress Control Number: 2016912075

Because of the dynamic nature of the Internet, any web addresses or links contained in
this book may have changed since publication and may no longer be valid. The views
expressed in this work are solely those of the author and do not necessarily reflect the
views of the publisher, and the publisher hereby disclaims any responsibility for them.

Any people depicted in stock imagery provided by Thinkstock are models,
and such images are being used for illustrative purposes only.
Certain stock imagery © Thinkstock.

Lulu Publishing Services rev. date: 07/28/2016

Contents

Preface

All these events are based on my own experiences. All the characters are real people. The unlawful events mentioned are listed in state police records.

I'm now semiretired. As a certified addiction professional, crisis intervention specialist, court/criminal-justice liaison, and motivational speaker, I still work with people who suffer from addictions. Along with my certifications, my own life experiences, strengths, and hopes are my best tools in helping others.

I've been a therapeutic-community former resident employed in that setting for thirty-eight years. For ways to help your child become drug-free, I highly recommend the book *You Can't Do It Alone* by Monsignor William O'Brien and Ellis Henican. If I can recover from making poor choices and overcome too many years of addiction, so can anyone else.

Acknowledgments

The Daytop residential addiction-treatment and rehabilitation program in Connecticut turned my life around and introduced me to a better and happier existence. I'm eternally grateful to its cofounders, Monsignor William O'Brien and psychiatrist Dr. Dan Casriel, and to its many directors and staff members—including, but by no means limited to, David Deitch, Ron Broncato, and Charles Devlin—who oversaw the operations at this facility and were vital to my receiving the most beneficial treatment.

Also influential to my recovery were those who relocated from the Daytop Swan Lake facility to the Connecticut residential facility, including George Tocci and director Kenny Williams, as well as Daytop's Connecticut residents, including Vinny Nuzzo and Jackie Robinson Jr. Thanks also to my mentor, King Dyckman, PhD; James Downey, uncle to Robert Downey Jr.; authors Jim Naughton and Larry Kudlow, who encouraged me to write; the men's fellowship group in Stratford, Connecticut; and the directors of the Connecticut Board of Pardons, Connecticut Renaissance drug-treatment center, Greater Bridgeport Regional Narcotic Programs, and Élan Corporation.

Thanks as well to my many childhood friends, including Denny Tillison, Vinny Knapp, Al Ambrose, Fred Kurtz, and all my friends from East Hartford High School.

I have been blessed with parents and sisters who were there for me in good and bad times. My daughter, Uriela, has been the greatest blessing in my life, and I thank her for the graphic design for the cover of *Blessed with Two Lives*.

Introduction

Reality therapy states that everyone is responsible for his or her own behavior—not society, not the environment, not heredity, not the past, but each individual. I have learned that addiction recovery involves teaching people how to look at what they have been doing, evaluate their own behavior, and make a plan to do better. Contentment with oneself and one's life does not come through a textbook or a magic solution to one's problems. It is attained by accepting responsibility for what one does instead of looking for blame or finding fault or dwelling on the past or feeling sorry for oneself. It requires a desire for improvement within the reality of one's own situation. It is about life and the way you live with yourself and others. This was Daytop's version of reality therapy, used in group sessions at the time.

Addiction to alcohol and drugs affects thousands of people in all walks of life. Because addiction can always return, there must be continued treatment. Freedom from addiction comes through involvement in a fellowship of men and women who keep showing each other by example how to say sober and clean. Treatment centers help in this process of changing negative attitudes and behaviors.

I've seen this therapy work for thousands, young and old, who suffer from addictions. One must be open-minded, willing to change, and dedicated to succeed through recovery. My story is about change, recovery, and redemption from addiction, negative behaviors, and criminal activities, through a higher power and the power of example from others who have changed and showed me the way out of addiction.

Chapter 1

Here I Am

My first life began on August 31, 1944, in Hartford, Connecticut. I was born with volvuluses, which are kinks or knots in the bowels. The same medical condition had killed my brother at his birth six years before mine. I required immediate, major abdominal surgery. Although the doctors explained I would definitely die without it, my mother was afraid to let them go ahead. She finally gave in after they repeatedly assured her there was a strong chance I would survive, but only if I had the surgery.

After my surgery and recovery, the doctors told my parents that the only reason I survived was because I was heavy at birth (12.3 pounds) and the extra weight had been essential to my survival. My brother, who had perished from the same disorder, had only been 7.5 pounds when he was born.

My recovery at home required a lot of care. I was unable to sleep on my stomach and had to be watched twenty-four hours a day for quite some time. While my father worked to support the family, my mother took care of me with assistance from my older sisters, who weren't yet old enough to go to school.

The surgery left me with a scar from the top of my rib cage all the way down to my belly button, and to this day I'm self-conscious about the disfigurement. (When I was older, I learned that movie star Farrah Fawcett had the same surgery, which explained why there was never a picture of her in a two-piece bathing suit.) When I went to the beach, people would stare at me, and kids would actually come up to me and ask what happened. As I got older, I'd lie and say a shark had bitten me or—depending on who had asked—that I had been shot or stabbed.

Now this is no longer an issue for me. I grew up with this scar and never knew any difference in my appearance. Besides, women have told me that scars have more character and more interesting stories than tattoos, which is always an ego-booster.

Chapter 2

The Family Years

I have several memories of my childhood, one of which is of being potty-trained. My mother would take off my diaper, put shorts on me, and tell me to play in the back, which was fenced-in and grassy. I had young friends living next door to me on both sides, and they made fun of me and made me cry even more.

The neighborhood and the community were built during World War II, and they were tough projects. Our home was situated in Mayberry Village in East Hartford, Connecticut, and the area was as poor and unsafe—as was our prior neighborhood of Charter Oak Terrace in Hartford, Connecticut.

I recall one day when I accidentally pooped in my pants. I was three years old, and once again, my friends made fun of me and made me cry. When I went to the door to tell my mother, she yelled at me, abruptly removed my pants, filled the sink with water, placed me into it, and continued to yell and spank me. I already believed my parents didn't want me or love me, so this incident merely supported my resentment against them and all authority figures.

My first encounter with the police came when I was five years old. Preferring the company of older kids, I'd stand with them at the corner of the entrance to our housing community and throw snowballs at the passing cars. One of the kids packed snow around a rock, and so I did, too. Without looking closely at the vehicle, I threw the rock snowball at a police car, and it cracked the window.

We all immediately ran. Since I was a younger and smaller child, I was unable to run as fast as the other kids, and so I was caught. The police took me home, and the next thing I recall was my mother yelling for me to come to the kitchen table and listen to her read a letter stating that we would have to go to juvenile court. Besides spanking and slapping me, she threatened to send me to boarding school. In court, the judge lectured me for some time and warned me that I was never to return to his court ever again. I never did go back to that courtroom, but as my life progressed, I would visit many others.

Another strongly remembered and oft-repeated incident from my youth occurred when I was six. My mother would drop me off at the neighborhood's little red schoolhouse, and I would immediately sneak out the rear of the school and race to our house so that I would be sitting there upon my mother's return from work. Every time, a truant officer would come to the door and report me for truancy. I hated that guy. He was very mean to all the kids, and he would manhandle us when he caught us.

At seven or eight years old, I was introduced to the game of playing "doctor" with the older girls in the community. One day, a bunch of us were in the woods along the Hockanum River in back of Labor Field. We played a game where all of our clothing was removed and all of us boys very graphically presented our penises to the girls. It was fun until we heard someone scream, "What the hell are you kids doing?" Lo and behold, it was my mother! I froze while all the other kids ran. My mom broke off a tree branch and very forcefully spanked me with it. I felt so bad and ashamed in front of my mother for doing what I knew was wrong.

The next incident I recall was at age ten when I fell through the ice, almost drowning and freezing to death. My mother had told me not to go onto the frozen ice covering the pond in the cove of the Hockanum River because it was already starting to melt on the sides and wasn't safe. So of course, I did the opposite. My friend Moe and I crawled out on a tree limb over the cove and lowered ourselves onto the middle of the pond to slide along the ice on our stomachs. We played for a while and then, as I was sliding off to the side, I fell through the ice.

I grabbed onto the ice to pull myself up, but the edges of the hole just kept breaking off in my hands. I could feel the current pulling at my legs, trying to suck me under. I kept fighting hard and screaming for help. Somehow, Moe was able to get off the ice and run for help. Two older men who were passing by yelled to me, "Drown, you little motherfucker. Drown!" And then they just laughed and walked away.

Soon my mother, my sister, my sister's boyfriend, and Moe came to the pond, but they couldn't get to me. The fire department arrived, and for a half hour they tried to figure out how to remove me from the water. Finally Moe, afraid to get back onto the ice, suggested to my sister's boyfriend that he might be able to use the same method we had. So my sister's brave boyfriend lay down on his stomach and slowly slid toward me. After a bit, he reached me, grabbed me by my collar, pulled me out, and dragged my tired body to safety.

Once home, I was immediately immersed into a tub full of hot water. I was so cold that my skin had a purple hue. A neighbor brought a glass filled with a brown liquid, and I was told that, although it might burn, I had to drink all of it. It looked just like prune juice, but it burned my mouth and throat and numbed my lips. And then, my body instantly began to warm. I later learned that she'd had me drink Four Roses bourbon whiskey. Little did any of us know, it would be that association and awareness of feeling good after drinking alcohol that would start me on my twenty-nine-year journey down a path of alcohol addiction.

Other memorable incidents in my young life were lightning strikes. Once while we were working in the tobacco fields, a thunderstorm started. There were around fourteen kids working at the time. We all had to run into a barn, and then a lightning strike came in the door of the barn. We all were burned and paralyzed. Several kids were rushed to the hospital, but in the end, all of us were okay.

One time, my mother was taking us home from a Spring Pond swimming trip. *Bang!* A bolt of lightning hit the car and pushed us off the road. We were shaken up, but we were okay. God had other plans for me.

Chapter 3

The Addictions and Crimes Begin

My friend Moe's father was an alcoholic. Every night, he'd drink almost an entire half pint of Schenley whiskey plus close to a six-pack of Rheingold beer and pass out. Moe would hide anything his father hadn't finished, so when we went to ballgames, parties, or just get-togethers with friends, we'd have something to drink. We thought we were so cool.

Needless to say, our consumption increased over time. One night, we needed a ride to a dance in Hartford. After drinking for a while, I decided to steal a bus at the local garage near my home. So I did. I picked up some of my drinking buddies, and off to the dance in the bus we went. After the dance, I drove back to East Hartford, dropped off my buddies, and returned the bus. This was so exciting to me—driving a big bus and not feeling any fear about what could have happened. At this time, I was going on fifteen and acting like a twenty-five-year-old. My friends thought I was crazy cool and full of fun.

By the time I turned fifteen, I was committing crimes like stealing cars and breaking and entering into restaurants and warehouses. I had also started hanging around with older kids who were committing crimes as well. I recall one incident in particular.

Jimmy Lata and his cohorts had been stealing hubcaps to sell, and I joined them. One time, we were caught and all taken to a police station. The other kids were arrested because they were older than sixteen, but I, being underage, was only detained while my father was called to come and get me. On the ride home, he tried to reason with me about the dangers of hanging out with such a group. Of course, I ignored his advice. Jimmy and his cohorts turned out to be very dangerous people—murderers and bank robbers among them. They slowly killed each other off.

One late evening, I came home drunk to find my father waiting up for me. He asked if I was drunk, even though the answer was obvious. Nonetheless, I denied it. My dad, a stiff-upper-lipped Englishman, hit me for the first time and gave me a beating. I just took it; I didn't dare hit him back. Besides, I respected him too much to do that. I felt I got what was due me. This would be the only time he ever raised a hand to me. Instead, for the rest of his life, he tried to reason with me and guide me.

I did stop drinking for a time. The problem was that I replaced alcohol with drugs—and then soon afterward, I went back to drinking as well, because I found my brother's birth certificate showing a date of birth six years prior to mine. I was looking in my parents' dresser drawer and found that birth certificate. It magically made me a twenty-one-year-old, and now I could buy booze and go into bars. *What a score!* I thought.

At the age of fifteen, I used that birth certificate to buy alcohol—and, of course, immediately became everybody's friend. I also began using heavier drugs, such as heroin, cocaine, and morphine. At the instigation of these new "friends," I robbed my first drugstore. My addiction to drugs and alcohol even induced me to rob Harlem drug dealers with sawed-off shotguns. After doing this, we could never go back to that block for fear of getting killed.

At that time, I was dating a high school cheerleader—a senior who had a boyfriend. I thought I was so cool. The day after her prom, an older friend gave me the use of his gray, primer-sprayed 1949

Ford Raked. I picked up Moe and several other neighborhood kids who I considered friends at the time, and we drove to Misquamicut Beach in Rhode Island. With my brother's birth certificate, I bought alcohol, and we partied on the beach and got drunk. At one point, we ran out of booze and money to buy more, so Moe and I decided we'd simply rob someone on the beach.

The next thing I knew, I was waking up in a jail cell with Moe next to me. Neither of us could recall the circumstances that had brought us there. An officer came and took me to meet with a suited detective in an office. The detective told me that Moe and I had driven away from the scene of a crime. Apparently, with Moe in the front passenger's seat, I drove off the road into someone's backyard and hit a senior man lying in his hammock. The man was in the hospital in critical condition and wasn't expected to live.

At my admission of not recalling anything that had happened, the detective told me that if I killed someone while committing a crime, I could be charged with murder. I was full of fear and remorse, crying and feeling so bad that this happened. None of my friends were around; they must have gotten rides home. No more cheerleader girlfriend; she didn't want anything to do with me. Until it became known whether the man would live, Moe and I were sent to Rhode Island School for Boys, where we remained for a year (my parents dutifully visiting me once a month) until we learned that the senior citizen would be able to live a relatively healthy life. Moe and I were both put on probation, and I was told that I could never drive in the state of Rhode Island again, with or without a driver's license.

Almost immediately after our court appearance, my addiction to drugs progressed. Moe and I were again arrested. We had been buying Robitussin cough syrup with codeine from a drugstore in Springfield, Massachusetts, to get high—and, as we were leaving, Moe grabbed a bottle of phenobarbital. We were caught and arrested, and because we were now sixteen years old, the consequences became more serious.

Moe's father hired a lawyer, and Moe was placed on probation. My father bonded me out with the intention of sending me to an addiction rehab facility. At the time, there were only two such facilities in the United States. The one in Lexington, Kentucky, ran television ads touting it as being the "cure." The other was in Fort Worth, Texas. In both places, you could only leave upon approval of the parent or court that sent you there. I was told that if I was accepted, a doctor would prescribe morphine to halt my urge to steal and use heroin until I actually entered rehab.

My friends Les and Donnie suggested I agree to go to the Lexington facility. I was now seventeen years old, with charges against me for drug possession and breaking and entering. I talked with my father about it, and he told me newsman Walter Winchell had called the facility a "forty-million-dollar flophouse in a federal prison." Upon acceptance, I was told that I'd be there for the minimum six-month stay.

Chapter 4

My First Time at Rehab

Upon arrival at the Lexington rehab center, I was placed in a room and given drugs to assist with detox. After the first dose of detox meds, I began feeling as bad as I've ever felt. It was an overall awful feeling physically, with the shakes, a splitting headache, and pains in my arms and legs that hurt so much I had to punch my legs and arms hard just to feel a different type of pain. Watery eyes, stomach aches, fluids coming out of every place they could, weak knees and legs, and pain all through my body—and to think, this was just one of many detoxes to come.

There was a research department on another level, and everyone was given Class A narcotics in order to determine the type of withdrawal he or she would experience. There was also an area with a group of monkeys that were given cocaine in liquid form to put them through forced detox and observe their withdrawals. After going through detox just once, the monkeys refused the cocaine, showing they were smarter than humans, who would not stop.

During my time in that facility, I met former drug dealers from all over the United States. On Saturday nights, we had talent shows that would include famous people, such as jazz drummer Philly Joe Jones. Even Johnny Cash and his wife would occasionally check in for brief recovery therapy. This was some experience for me at a very young age. In a way, this was not the best place for me to spend six months, meeting older drug addicts and learning more ways to steal, get high, and act out. I had no idea what was ahead of me in this way of life.

Upon my release after six months, I was put on a train for New York with two rehabilitated junkies—a man and a woman who were from the city. As soon as we got off the train, the man immediately said, "Let's cop some drugs and get high."

The woman said, "Not me. I'm going to a bar for a drink."

When the man looked my way, I nodded and went with him. We bought a forty-dollar spoonful of heroin and snuck into an apartment building's unlocked basement bathroom to get high. Looking over at me, he cocked his head and said that I looked pretty young. He asked if I had ever shot dope before. I reassured him that I had a lot of experience with the stuff. He then took some water out of the toilet tank to cook up the heroin. Both of us sat down on the floor and leaned against the wall to enjoy the high. He quickly passed out, and I almost did, too. I tried to bring him back to consciousness, but I couldn't, so I left him there and caught a train back home to Hartford. At Penn Station, I couldn't find the locker where I had put all my stuff when I arrived in New York, so I just left everything there.

I telephoned my father, and he picked me up. Under the impression that I had been "cured," he told me that I'd received a sentence of five years in Wethersfield State Prison, suspended, with two years' probation. I was only seventeen, but five years in prison sounded like it might as well have been twenty. One of my older friends had been given a sentence of five years just for being in possession of one marijuana joint, and another friend had received seven years for stealing a doctor's bag. It was 1961, and doctors' bags were easy to steal because their car license plate indicated who they were, and they'd often leave their bags in their cars. As a last resort, my friends and I would break into doctors' cars to steal the bag to get the drugs inside.

Chapter 5

The Reformatory

Come 1962, I was arrested yet again. Although I had been driving perfectly, I was recognized by the police and pulled over (this was before the Miranda Act was in effect, and cops could randomly pull anyone over). Turns out one of my passengers had drugs with him and, too naïve to know better, stuffed them under the front seat. The cops searched all of us as well as the car and, of course, found the drugs. The friend denied the drugs were his and told the cops I was just driving him home. So I was arrested again, with probation for a five-year suspended sentence hanging over my head.

I was looking at drug-related crimes that included larceny, possession of narcotics, and violation of probation. The case seemed to drag on, but finally I received my punishment. Because I was still seventeen, I was sentenced to two to five years in Cheshire Reformatory instead of Wethersfield State Prison. Inside, I not only saw several friends, but I made new ones. Over time, I would learn that many of these kids died untimely and premature deaths.

Cheshire Reformatory was for boys ages sixteen to twenty-one, and it was run very similar to the home for boys in the movie *Sleepers,* in which the young residents were tortured and sexually assaulted by sadistic guards. A lot of abuse took place in Cheshire Reformatory as well. By the time I entered, there had already been a riot at the institution because of the years of abuse the young prisoners were forced to endure. Billy-club and blackjack beatings of the kids had been widespread—to control behaviors, or just out of cruelty. Guards would also sexually abuse boys who appeared frail or gay, and these children had no choice but to comply.

The riot, in which guards as well as inmates were cut up, just made things worse. I knew I could never let my guard down. I not only had to look and act tough but *be* tough, if needed. I saw guards repulsively manipulate boys by threatening them with segregation and being locked up unless they consented. Sometimes I even saw kids trade sex with the guards for candy and cigarettes. In 1974, just a little more than ten years after I was discharged, I learned that the Cheshire

Reformatory had beaten a kid to death who was living for quite some time in a single cell far away from the other children. An investigation led to the removal of clubs and blackjacks, and ultimately Cheshire Reformatory, once a prison for kids, was converted into a prison that treated its inmates as if they were at a country club.

After serving fifteen months, I was released in December of 1963 into a time of radical and rebellious social change. Citizens and militants worldwide were protesting and demonstrating about every possible issue imaginable, including ethnic prejudice, gender unfairness and injustice, religious freedom, and the Vietnam war. These issues carried deep, heartfelt emotions of sorrow, pain, guilt, and anger that often resulted in harm, killings, and assassinations. During this time, most people judged each other by what movement they were involved in. As for me, I rebelled against the rebellious.

I returned to living with my family in the projects of Mayberry Village in East Hartford, Connecticut. I also returned to using alcohol and drugs regularly. I was satisfied with my drug-induced existence; I had no desire whatsoever for it to be interrupted by the world's issues.

A few months later in early 1964, at age twenty, I married Betty, a woman I met at a local dance club who was my first of three wives.

We were bad for each other, so we divorced after a few years. My second wife, Maritza, was the woman with whom I had my longest relationship. We were together for seventeen years, had one child, and are very good friends today. My third wife, Pamela, was a lot of fun. We traveled; went to concerts, plays, and movies; and enjoyed each other's company. It ended after several years together.

Pamela was a big Prince fan. We went to a few of his concerts together in New York City. She knew him and the band well; she traveled the globe going to his concerts. We were both very sad that he was addicted to drugs and died that way, in so much pain. Another great dies of an OD of prescription drugs. May he rest in peace.

Chapter 6

The Summer of 1965

Along with my friends Richie and Jeb, I started using drugs heavily. Whenever we ran out of narcotics and were desperate for more, we'd simply hook up with a local drugstore-robbing gang. During the daytime, we'd size up drugstores outside of our area to see where they kept their narcotics (drug cabinets would either be leaning against a back wall, screwed into a wall, or behind the pharmacy counter). Other times, one of us would go into the bathroom, climb up into the rafters, and hide there until the last employee left. We'd wait until a police car performed its drive-by check. If none of us was already in the store hiding, we'd wait ten minutes and break in by going through the front plate-glass windows. Even if the store had an alarm, we'd be in and out within three minutes.

Drugstores made for easy targets, and we could also grab all the money, cigarettes, wristwatches, and anything else we could during those three minutes. There were several different crews hitting drugstores during this time period, mostly from Hartford. During the mid-sixties, there were well over fifty drugstores in Connecticut, Massachusetts and Rhode Island that had been robbed of narcotics.

One very hot day in June 1965, my addict buddies Jeb and Rizzo and I were feeling weak and nauseous because we had run out of drugs. At the street-experienced age of twenty, we knew that some crews would trade or sell to each other if one group had a lot of cocaine or morphine and another needed drugs for its customers. So I came up with the idea of stealing from a guy on one of these crews who we knew fairly well who had a stash in the basement of his mother's house in Hartford.

We first telephoned to make sure no one was home and were encouraged when the phone just rang and rang. I had been there the evening before, so I knew where he kept the stash. We broke in through the cellar door, made our way though a dusty rat-infested basement full of spiderwebs, and grabbed his stash of cocaine and morphine. We had a nice supply of heroin and cocaine (Class 1 narcotics), each bottle bearing a skull and crossbones to indicate the contents were considered poisonous. Finding a reclusive area off the main street, we immediately shot up cocaine mixed with morphine (speedballs) and Dilaudid. Jeb started eating Dolophines (dolphin tabs) as if they were M&Ms. In no time, the three of us were feeling good again.

We got in the car and started to drive home, but we were too high to make it all the way to East Hartford. We stopped at the Manchester Motel in the next town. Rizzo's phony ID had rented us the car, and now it rented us a room. Jeb was too high to do anything except nod out. Rizzo and I considered going out to get some food, but then we recalled that we'd probably throw up, which was a likely thing to do even with something as light as ice cream or a milkshake. So we decided to instead split up the drugs three ways, knowing full well we'd be shortchanging the passed-out Jeb. Afterward, Rizzo and I continued to do some more drugs, and eventually we too nodded out.

Morning came, and I was the only one awake. I saw that the other guys were completely out of it. I put some cold water and ice on Rizzo's face, slapping his cheeks lightly until he came around. Then Rizzo and I went to do the same with Jeb, but we saw that he was breathing heavily and fluids were running out of his nose and mouth. This was a definite indication of an overdose. We put cold towels on his head and neck, under his arms, and on his testicles. No response.

We then injected saltwater into his veins. Again, nothing. Rizzo and I became frightened. I tried mouth-to-mouth resuscitation, even though Jeb's coloring was already turning from gray to blue. I blew the last breath into his mouth, and he let out his last breath. He was dead.

Rizzo and I were terrified and panicky, but finally we came up with a plan. First, we'd gather up all the drugs, and Rizzo would hide them somewhere. Then he'd go to a particular phone booth we used whenever we were in the area, of which we knew the phone number. We'd say that Rizzo was waiting to hear from Jeb upon awakening to find out what he wanted Rizzo to pick up for breakfast. Then I'd tell the police that I was unable to awaken Jeb.

When the ambulance and police arrived, I rattled off our story really fast and stood outside the room and watched, hoping they'd revive him. Although deep inside I knew he was dead, I still didn't want to believe it. A few moments later, the ambulance staff conferred with the police, and it was only a few minutes later that a medical examiner arrived and pronounced Jeb dead. I was immediately handcuffed, led to a police car, and pushed face down into the back seat. Locked up in the Manchester Police Station and unaware the police had already picked up Rizzo at the phone booth for questioning, I told them the story Rizzo and I had concocted.

Hours passed before I was brought to a detective's office. I asked why I was being held and whether I was under arrest. I was informed that both Rizzo and I were under arrest for possession of illegal narcotics (found under the dashboard of the car, where Rizzo had decided he would "hide" them) and maybe also for murder. He said they had witnesses who heard Rizzo and me talking the night before about killing Jeb over drugs and money.

Could things get any worse? Apparently, yes. Because I had served the two-to-five-year sentence in 1963 in Cheshire Reformatory and was on parole, I couldn't make bond. So I was soon off to the old Syms Street county jail in Hartford. I made the front page of the *Hartford Courant*, the largest daily newspaper in the entire state of Connecticut.

The investigation took months. They spoke with several friends in our neighborhood and even some from our crew. A detective questioned a female friend of ours who said that at a party the night before, I had threatened to kill Jeb. I tried to explain that while I did say that, it was just a figure of speech and that friends say that to each other all the time without a second thought of actually doing it. The detective said that I still might be charged with murder, and I shrieked, "No fucking way!"

His response? "Watch and see."

And so, there I was, newly twenty-one, facing a murder charge and the threat of going to Osborn State Prison in Somers, Connecticut.

Rizzo and I remained in Syms Street jail for the rest of the summer. When fall began, his family came up with a bond for him and he left. The facility was awful. There were no toilets in the cells, and only a bucket was available for use after lights went out at night. Then we'd have to empty and rinse the bucket each day, so the intention became not to use it. But some others cells didn't mind, and all night the entire block of cells stunk.

During the time that Rizzo was still in there with me, detectives would come from all around the state to question us about drugstores that were robbed, because they wanted to clear up their books. We were told that if we would confess to these robberies, we could avoid charges of murder or manslaughter.

To pass our time in jail during the daytime, I would play cards with a bizarre man by the name of Walter. He was always fighting and getting high, and he had been in jail for most of his young life. Tensions would rise between Rizzo and us, and we'd find ourselves fighting with our fists over a card game. Then, drugs were easy to access—still the case in jails today, apparently—he and I would get high and we'd be friends again. This happened over and over again. After Rizzo was released on bond, I learned that his story kept changing about the events leading to Jeb's death and that the detectives believed that I was the one who supplied the drugs. Therefore, I was responsible for Jeb's death.

I was eventually assigned a public defender for the charge of narcotics possession and for parole violation of the sentence I had received in 1963. Thankfully, charges relating to Jeb's death were never mentioned or considered. We went back and forth to court for about six months, and I finally agreed to a sentence of one to five years in Osborn, with the dropping of the parole violation.

There I was, sentenced, handcuffed, and held in a cell waiting to go to prison. In a line with other convicts waiting to get onto the prison bus, I had leg cuffs and a chain locked around my waist. I could see my mother and father watching me—my father waving good-bye and my mother crying. I felt embarrassed and sorrowful for hurting them, but because I couldn't show weakness in front of the other prisoners, I sat expressionless. I was the only boy in my family. My two sisters, Alice and Carol, were angels and never got into any trouble. I, on the other hand, had only caused my family pain.

Chapter 7

Off to Prison

Seeing the bus with "Osborn Correctional Facility" painted on the side reminded me about one of its former prisoners, Harry Unsworth, whom I had known since I was a kid. Some of us who were close to him were aware he had an intimate relationship with a guy named Ware, but Harry really didn't want anyone to know, so it was never mentioned by anyone. Harry and Ware were in prison at the same time, and one day our neighborhood got word that Ware had disappeared. When Harry was released, I commented to him that I hadn't seen Ware around, and Harry replied, "He's stiff. In cement." Harry didn't go into more detail, and I knew better than to ask.

After Harry got out of jail, he threatened to shoot me a couple of times because he had fronted some money and drugs to me and

I was having a hard time paying him back. Then, one day, I heard on the radio that a man in Woodbridge, Connecticut, had been found shot to death gangland style, still slumped over the steering wheel of his car. Because of the location, Harry immediately came to mind. Later, the news announced the name of the victim, and sure enough, it was Harry. At that time, I still had a lot of the drugs he'd fronted to me as well as some of his counterfeit money. I considered them a gift.

Also on the bus to Osborn was a man going back to prison on violation of parole charges. He called himself Cheating Charlie. He was quite a con man and very funny, but something about him made me uncomfortable. He was the first prisoner I spoke with one-on-one, though, and I knew I needed to befriend him regardless of whether I felt at ease with him. I had been in prison before, and I was well aware of how I was supposed to act and whom to befriend or not.

Osborn was still fairly new when I arrived there in September of 1965, so the cells hadn't begun to really stink yet. The floors were heated. This facility felt like a palace compared to the hellhole of Syms Street jail.

Gang and crew members clearly identified themselves and hung out with each other in cliques, including the Hells Angels, Black

Panthers, Huns motorcycle group, Minute Men, Ku Klux Klan, and Muslims. Others would hang out with the "city" guys. Statistics indicate that the population in American prisons during that time period was 72 percent white, 27 percent black and 10 percent "other." Blacks and whites were segregated, with whites sitting in one dining room and blacks in another. Hispanics could choose to sit with either. Blacks served blacks and whites served whites. Only when the segregated lines were uneven in number would the guards even them out. Sometimes I was chosen to eat with the black population, and I never encountered any problems doing so.

There were so many characters in prison. One was Bobby M., a wild young guy with eyes that crossed so severely that inmates and guards alike could never tell exactly where he was looking. Bobby had been imprisoned for several crimes, one of which was robbing banks. We talked about why I was in prison, and he couldn't understand the need for imprisonment of someone using drugs. He said it had to do with the state making money on each prisoner.

He then talked about his history. He said that he was part of a Connecticut crew that, according to the FBI, was "the biggest bank robbery gang in the US" during the sixties. He explained in clear detail how the robberies occurred. After splitting the money, he'd go to Vegas and gamble, drink, and hire call girls until his money ran out. He and his buddies would get busted on a regular basis. They'd get out, rob another bank, get caught, and go back to prison.

One time, Bobby M. and I were playing handball in the gym with a carton of cigarettes as the stakes. He was strongly focused when a basketball from the other end of the gym rolled into our game area. He grabbed the ball and threw it back, yelling, "Keep that fucking ball outa here!" After a few repeats of this same scenario, he snapped. He picked up the ball, charged across the floor, and threw the ball into the face of the biggest guy standing there. And then, the fight began. Soon, the guards pounced on both and took them away. Personally, that was fine with me. Bobby M. was beating me in our handball game anyway.

Several years later, Bobby would be found in the trunk of a car in East Hartford shot to death gangland style.

A few weeks after I arrived at Osborn, Mookie arrived. He also lived in the projects and had been a close friend of mine. He and I would rob people and stores and use drugs together. In fact, he had been the best man at my first wedding. A heavyweight champ while he was in the navy, he was looked up to by everybody. Although he was one of the toughest guys I had ever known, there were some guys who still challenged him. I once saw him punch a guy and actually knock the guy's eyeball out with a right hook. I never knew of anyone ever beating Mookie. His reputation protected me when we were kids on the street, and he protected me in prison as well.

One day, Mookie heard that an inmate by the name of Jimmy C. took a swing at me while I was working in the prison kitchen because I asked him why he punched my friend Frank. Although Jimmy C. was slow on his feet and I was able to hold him at bay, Mookie gathered a few tough inmates with homemade shanks (knives), and we waited in the hallway leading to a small yard. Mookie had instructed us that as soon as we saw Jimmy C. come down the hallway, we were to stab and kill him for "fucking with Hartford boys."

I was scared to death. I was doing a one-to-five-year bid and just wanted to go home afterward, not end up with a life sentence for murder. Thankfully, Jimmy C. never did come down the hallway that night, and things cooled off—but not before two guys said they hated him and asked Mookie and I to come to New Haven when we were released so that we could help kill him. Mookie and I were contacted after our release, but we both said we were busy and couldn't make it. We later learned that Jimmy C. was killed and thrown off a highway overpass, after which he was run over a few times.

Another fellow prisoner was New Haven's most infamous mobster, Salvatore "Midge Renault" Annunziato, who was called Miggie by those close to him. On Sunday afternoons, he and I, along with several other inmates, would watch the football game while drinking Canadian Club whiskey and taking Black Beauty methamphetamine pills. Miggie would regale us with stories about his life of crime without giving too many details, but we already knew a lot from gossip and what we had read in the newspapers. After Miggie's release, he became too cocky and in mid-1979 simply disappeared.

ASSOCIATED PRESS

From left: Actor Dylan McDermott, his mother, Diane McDermott, and her boyfriend John Sponza. Waterbury police reopened the investigation last year into Diane McDermott's 1967 death after Dylan McDermott contacted them with questions.

1967 CASE REOPENED

Police: Boyfriend killed Dylan McDermott's mother

WATERBURY (AP) — A reopened police investigation has concluded that actor Dylan McDermott's mother was killed in 1967 by her now-dead gangster boyfriend.

Waterbury police reopened the investiga-tion last year into Diane McDermott's death after Dylan McDermott contacted them with questions, the Republican-American newspaper reported Sunday and Monday as part of a two-part series.

McDermott was 5 years old when his mother was shot in February 1967. Her death was originally ruled an accident.

Police told the newspa-per that the evidence they found would be enough to file murder charges

See Actor's on A3

nother murdered in 1967

in the trunk of a car in a Waltham, Mass., grocery store parking lot.

The state's medical ex-aminer, H. Wayne Carver, reviewed McDermott's autopsy and determined that the gun found near the body was too small a caliber to have been the weapon used to kill her.

that the murder weapon had been pressed to the back of her head, accord-ing to his report.

Dylan McDermott, who won a Golden Globe in 1999 for his role on the TV drama "The Practice," declined to comment about the investigation.

His sister, Robin Herre-

truth has been discovered

"I'm happy to know my mother wasn't mentally ill or depressed," she said. "Somebody took her from us; she didn't leave us."

Police said the McDer-mott investigation has led to evidence that also implicates Sponza in at least two other unsolved

Also in prison at the same time was Johnny Sponza, whom I had met when I was in Cheshire Reformatory. A tough wiseguy who said his life aspiration was to be a gangster, he had been the primary suspect in the 1967 murder of actor Dylan McDermott's mother. Johnny met the same demise as Bobby—in the trunk of a car.

Although getting through this jail sentence was difficult, it was bearable because Rizzo had been sentenced here for possession of narcotics and violation of probation. Once again we were able to get high together. If a prisoner had money, drugs could be purchased from the guards, and Miggie and his crew were able to get anything they wanted. Rizzo and I became good friends with them.

One night, I went to my cell because I was too high to continue socializing in the recreation area. Rizzo, on the other hand, continued taking more and more pills, getting higher and higher. He stopped by my cell and could hardly continue standing. I told him he should hurry back to his cell before he was busted, but he just kept talking. It wasn't until shortly afterward when a bell rang indicating that everyone had to get back to his cell for "cell count" that Rizzo finally left.

Soon afterward, I returned to the common television area and sat watching television with Miggie and others, drinking Canadian Club whiskey. There was the usual background traffic that drowned out the volume of any show we were watching. Guards changed at midnight, and often there was shuffling by the medical staff wheeling out some inmate who had been severely cut in a fight or who killed himself.

This night, an inmate was wheeled by in a body bag. We asked if it was someone from our cell block, and the guard looked right at me and said, "It's your buddy Rizzo. He OD'd."

I was numb. Between the alcohol and the shock of the body being Rizzo's, I was completely immobile, and I remained numb about it for several months—until one day, about six months later, I was called to the chapel to speak with the prison priest. I assumed the priest wanted to know why I hadn't attended services on Sunday during those months, but after he brought me into his office and directed me to sit down, he softly told me that my father had died. I felt like I had been punched in the stomach by the toughest guy in the prison. I recalled my parents' visit the weekend before. My dad had asked me, "Are you holding on okay?" and I'd promised him that I would stop doing drugs.

I simply broke down and cried. It took some time for me to regain my composure, at which time the priest asked me if I wanted to attend the wake or funeral. At my choice, he said he would speak with the warden and arrange for me to attend the wake.

I was driven to the wake in a prison suit, wearing hand and ankle cuffs. Although all cuffs were removed before I entered the premises, the shame on everyone's face and in my heart when I walked through the door sat heavily in the air.

I would learn that my father had driven to the local drive-in theatre and hooked a hose from the car's exhaust pipe into the inside of his car through the window. He had died of carbon monoxide poisoning. My father had committed suicide, and this time I felt like I was punched in the stomach by God himself. I heard he left a suicide note. I've never seen it—I think my sisters didn't want me to. I feel that it had something to do maybe with me. I had guilty feelings for years until I resolved them in therapy and rehab.

Chapter 8

Entering Daytop

I was released early from Osborn Correctional Facility in July of 1969. Although I had always been able to find drugs and alcohol while locked up, they were even more easily accessible on the streets, and so my addiction not only continued but grew. The drugs certainly helped to silence the pain of the loss of my father and my best friend, Rizzo. Soon, though, my need for drugs and alcohol far outweighed my ability to pay for them, and in 1970, some drug dealers to whom I owed quite a large amount of money put a contract out on my life.

Although I tried to lay low, I was arrested yet again, with charges and sentencing pending. As I agonized over the choice between being killed or going back to prison, my attorney suggested the Daytop addiction-treatment and recovery program at its Connecticut location. I learned that in 1957, New York priest Father William O'Brien, disturbed by the growing issue of drug and alcohol addiction among urban youth, had founded Daytop Village with psychiatrist Daniel H. Casriel and social worker and criminologist Alexander Bassin. Originally a halfway house for convicted addicts, it had grown into a program with locations in forty-eight countries that revolutionized drug-treatment methods.

Daytop traced its origins back to an incident that occurred on July 30, 1957. Members of three of New York's most violent gangs arranged to meet in a city park for a "peace talk." What took place was far from peaceful. When all was done, one was dead and another lay dying. The bloodshed that took place ignited a firestorm of controversy surrounding the growing drug problem among urban youth. Alerted by the distraught mother of one of the gang members, Father O'Brien began to search for answers to this great problem. His work culminated in the founding of Daytop Village.

The public and professional perspective on drug abuse in the late 1950s and early 1960s was essentially "once a junkie, always a junkie." This belief was supported by prominent figures from government, medicine, and the psychiatric profession. An addict on the street cost society money because the addict stole to support his or her habit. If the individual was jailed, society had to pay for that too, but hospitalization offered little hope for recovery.

At this same time, in Santa Monica, California, a recovering alcoholic named Charles Dederich had established an informal center for the recovery of addicts that represented a radical departure from accepted psychiatric thinking. The central tools of Dederich's system, originally called "synanons" and later "games" or "group encounters," were meetings of eight or ten addicts who would confront every aspect of each other's character, demanding change for the better and attacking any reluctance to become a more mature adult.

Dederich's center became known as Synanon. Believing that his was the only system that could offer an addict relief from desperation, Dederich began to branch out. He opened a house in Westport, Connecticut, to serve as an introduction center for East Coast addicts. The house met with much hostility from local citizens, but nevertheless it began to operate with a small population. This was the birth of a movement.

Having heard of the remarkable success of the Synanon method, Father O'Brien went to Westport to experience Synanon firsthand. As he was coming to the entrance, he met Dr. Casriel, a noted psychiatrist who was also there to learn more about this curious new approach to drug treatment. Although both had planned to spend only a few hours, they were so excited by what they witnessed that they stayed through the night. They walked away from that chance meeting with a new relationship cemented by the hope that the question of drug addiction could be answered through the Synanon system.

Dr. Casriel was at the time a consulting psychiatrist for the probation department of the Kings County Supreme Court. He reported back that a possible solution to the revolving-door life of addict probationers had been found. Joseph Shelly, head of the department, was also seeking such a solution, and together with Casriel and Bassin, director of education and research for the department, he applied to the National Institute of Mental Health for a research grant.

After completing a fact-finding trip designed to evaluate programs already in practice, Shelly and his group developed a research project that compared the relative progress of drug addict probationers in three control groups: residents in halfway houses modeled after Synanon, members of a special probation caseload made up exclusively of addicts, and a control group of twenty-five addict probationers selected according to the standard geographically defined probation system. Their proposed method of evaluating success or failure was the use of thin-layer chromatography, a urinalysis system for detecting drug use.

They submitted their proposal to the Institute of Mental Health in April of 1963 and were awarded a $390,000 grant for a five-year research study. A contest was held among the employees of the probation department to coin a name for the halfway house, and the name Daytop was chosen, standing for "Drug Addicts Treated on Probation." To avoid the stigma of institutionalization, the new house was called Daytop Lodge. The search for a site led Shelly and his group to Butler Manor, an unoccupied mansion on Staten Island.

On September 1, 1963, Daytop Lodge opened its doors with a population of twenty-two male probationers. The first year of Daytop was marked by troubles. A Synanon graduate who had been selected as director was unable to wait during the months between announcement of the grant and selection of the site, and he had found other employment. The group then hired a member of Alcoholics Anonymous, hoping that the similarities between the two systems would outweigh the differences and that the gap might be bridged intuitively. This proved too difficult a task, and unable to handle the strain, that first director resigned.

By the late summer of 1964, Daytop Lodge had been through eleven directors, and the project seemed to be in serious trouble. During this time, Father O'Brien, who had moved from Manhattan to a parish in the Bronx, was actively championing this new set of ideas. He had been back to the Westport Synanon house and had formed a relationship with one of the directors, David Deitch. Eventually, Deitch left Synanon, and through his relationship with Father O'Brien and Dr. Casriel agreed to become the new director of Daytop Lodge.

With the hiring of Deitch, all the dormant potential of Daytop seemed to spring to life. Deitch—along with Ron Broncato, also a former member of Synanon—was able to create the social dynamic that had so excited Father O'Brien and Dr. Casriel during their first visit to the house in Westport. Shelly, Casriel, Deitch, and Father O'Brien then met with New York's Mayor Wagner to propose founding a nonprofit corporation to receive state and city funding for the purpose of establishing a new and larger Daytop. Called Daytop Village, it was incorporated in May of 1965. It would widen the circle of admissions to Daytop to include, beyond male probationers, referrals from the community and women. It would also include me.

On that day in 1970 when my options seemed so hopeless, I was given a printout of Daytop's philosophy:

> I am here because there is no refuge, finally from myself. Until I confront myself in the eyes and hearts of others, I am running. Until I suffer them to know my secrets, I have no safety from them. Afraid to be known, I can know neither myself nor any other, I will be alone. Where else but in our common ground, can I find such a mirror? Here, together, I can at last appear clearly to myself, not as a giant of my dreams, nor the dwarf of my fears, but as a person, part of the whole, with my share in its purpose. In this ground I can take root and grow, not alone any more, as in death, but alive to myself and to others.

I wrote to Daytop and requested approval to enter into its Seymour, Connecticut, facility. Because pretty much anyone was admitted who asked to participate, I was accepted.

On January 7, 1971, still enormously immature at age twenty-five, I entered Daytop. I was ushered into a living-room-like area and seated in what was called a "prospect chair" that faced the wall. Around me were many residents who were doing things like dusting and cleaning the room, writing, and reading. I was instructed not to even look at them, let alone talk to anyone. Instead, I was to stare at the wall while reflecting on my entire life, including what had brought me to be sitting in that chair.

I had no idea how long I had been sitting there, but after some time I started to become ill. Although I had taken 100 milligrams of Dolophine (methadone) before even walking into the building, I was feeling more and more uncomfortable. Added to that discomfort was that not one person had come over to me. I would later learn that I sat there for about seven hours and that some program participants sat for an entire day or two, being immediately returned to the chair after eating and sleeping.

Finally I was led into an interview room where several residents were sitting. I was asked what investment I was willing to make in order to go through the program. I became annoyed and sarcastically asked if they wanted me to cry out for help. Apparently, this was a common response by newcomers, because my reply was met with smiles. I was then told that I had to get on my hands and knees and move around the room, barking like a dog; otherwise, I had to go back to the prospect chair. It took me only moments to accept that I had to do what they ordered, so I got down on my hands and knees and barked. Before I knew it, tears were flowing down my face. My tough-guy exterior had been breached.

I was then told to stand up, and all of them came over and hugged me with tears flowing, welcoming me into the Daytop family. Although I was confused by this process, deep in my heart I knew it was the beginning of a new and better life.

DEAR MONSIGNOR O'BRIEN:

NANCY AND I ARE PLEASED TO JOIN IN ALL THE CONGRATU-
LATIONS YOU ARE RECEIVING ON THE 25TH ANNIVERSARY OF
THE FOUNDING OF DAYTOP. YOU CAN BE TRULY PROUD OF YOUR
QUARTER CENTURY OF COMMITMENT TO DRUG ABUSE TREAT-
MENT FOR YOUNG PEOPLE.

THE DRIVE FOR A DRUG-FREE AMERICA HAS ACQUIRED NEW
MOMENTUM IN RECENT YEARS, AND THE LONG-TERM DEDICA-
TION OF INDIVIDUALS LIKE YOU IS ONE OF THE MAJOR REASONS
WHY YOU AND THE FINE STAFF AND VOLUNTEERS OF DAYTOP
HAVE BEEN IN THIS BATTLE FROM THE BEGINNING, INSPIRING
OTHERS AND SHOWING THE WAY TO HOPE AND RECOVERY. THE
SUCCESS YOU'VE ACHIEVED IN TRAGEDIES AVERTED AND LIVES
RESTORED—YOUR PROGRAM HAS, I UNDERSTAND, SOME 50,000
GRADUATES—IS EXTRAORDINARY. GOOD NEWS TRAVELS FAST,
SO IT'S NO WONDER THEN THAT DAYTOP PROGRAMS HAVE BEEN
ESTABLISHED IN EUROPE AND ASIA AS WELL.

THE EXPERIENCE DAYTOP HAS GAINED IN REHABILITATION OF
DRUG USERS WILL BE OF INCREASING VALUE IN THE YEARS
AHEAD AS NEW PROGRAMS ARE INITIATED TO MEET THE UR-
GENT NEED. YOUNG PEOPLE CAUGHT IN THE SNARE OF SUB-
STANCE ABUSE MUST KNOW THAT OUR SOCIETY HAS NOT WRIT-
TEN THEM OFF AND NEVER WILL. THEY MUST BE ALLOWED TO
SEE THAT THE PATH BACK TO HEALTH AND A DRUG-FREE LIFE IS
OPEN, AND THAT IT IS LINED WITH PEOPLE READY TO OFFER
THEIR WISDOM AND SUPPORT FOR THE JOURNEY. YOU HAVE
HELPED SEVERAL GENERATIONS OF YOUTH TO JUST SUCH A RE-
ALIZATION, AND FOR THAT YOU HAVE THE ADMIRATION AND
PROFOUND THANKS OF ALL YOUR FELLOW CITIZENS.

AGAIN, CONGRATULATIONS ON THIS MILESTONE, AND MAY THE
FUTURE BE FILLED WITH EVEN GREATER REWARDS FOR THE
ENTIRE DAYTOP FAMILY. GOD BLESS YOU.

SINCERELY,

Ronald Reagan

Jackie Robinson, Jr.

Father, Number 42 Jackie Robinson, quotation on his father's tombstone reads: The only measure of life is the impact left on others

Chapter 9

The Daytop Program

When I entered Daytop, the program was structured with eighteen to twenty-four months of meetings, groups, seminars, and job functions, which gave residents very little free time to get into trouble. Its behavior modification program dealt with much more than drug addiction. All resident addicts had to accept that their negative beliefs, attitudes, and behaviors had to change, and it was going to be a long and difficult process.

There was a morning meeting every day. Three mandatory daily encounter groups dealt with distrust and anger toward family, friends, ourselves, one another, and the rest of the world. We were also required to attend a topic seminar every day.

There was a chain of command made up of former addicts with different levels of responsibility. Everyone had a job function to perform daily. An incoming resident would start with the service crew and clean everywhere in the facility that needed cleaning, then they'd advance to kitchen crew to prepare, serve, and clean up— followed by promotion to ram rod (directing the crews and making sure they accomplished their tasks) and finally to expediter (the eyes and ears of the program, making sure residents were performing their jobs and not doing anything they weren't supposed to be doing, such as smoking in nondesignated smoking areas). Expediters also checked sleeping areas for neatness and cleanliness. Everything in the entire facility had to be white-glove clean. With its Saturday room inspections, it felt like a military-style community.

One of the group leaders with whom I became close friends was Jackie Robinson Jr., son of the first black baseball player who broke the color barrier in the sport. Jackie Jr. taught other group leaders how to deal with the subjects of prejudice and racism and also acted as a community-relations representative, where he developed and engaged community involvement and support. He once connected with a friend of his father who was with the Chock Full O' Nuts Corporation and arranged for the company to donate, among other things, a bus to the Daytop program that was used for all resident transportation purposes. From time to time, he'd have picnics in Stanford, Connecticut, at the house where his parents lived, and the Daytop family was always invited. Jackie Jr.'s mother, Rachel, worked at Yale, with which Daytop was affiliated.

Jackie Jr. came to the rescue of our Daytop facility when fire inspectors said our buildings needed fire escapes. The city didn't want a drug program in town, and this was an issue that threatened Daytop's existence in Connecticut. Jackie went to New York and put together the Jackie Robinson Jazz Festival with appearances by the Reverend Jesse Jackson, Roberta Flack, and other stars to raise money for the costly fire escapes.

One night, on his way back to Daytop after leaving the Apollo Theater in New York, Jackie Jr. was involved in an accident on Merritt Parkway in Connecticut and was killed. The Daytop family was in shock, and I was devastated at losing a close and respected friend. My despair led me to question the purpose of recovery if dying like that followed. I angrily left the program after six and a half months and went back to Hartford. Even though I had been clean during my time at Daytop, I immediately bought some alcohol and a bag of heroin and went into the bathroom on the main floor of Saint Francis Hospital to shoot up. I remember waking up on a table in a hospital room and doctors saying, "He's coming around."

As soon as I straightened out, I left the hospital, brought my mother's car back to her, and called Daytop, asking them to take me back. After several days of begging and despite my bed having already been given to a new resident, I nonetheless was able to return to the facility—where I had my head shaved. The residents felt that since I had acted like a baby, I should look like one. I also had to start the program over again from scratch, returning to the prospect chair and enduring a general meeting in which my fellow residents relayed how upset and disappointed they felt about what I had done. Thus I was lovingly welcomed back.

I still faced court review and sentencing. Because of my past arrests and conviction record, I received a very heavy suspended sentence—two ten- to twenty-year sentences, to run consecutively. The other alternative, the court stated, was that I could be placed on five years' probation if I continued toward completion of Daytop's eighteen- to twenty-four-month program.

In August 1972, I graduated from the Daytop program and was presented with a decision. I could move out and get a job, or I could stay on as a paid staff trainee. It was an easy decision. Because Daytop had guided me to kick my addictions and desire for drugs of any kind, I decided to take the position and the provided room and board. Now, though, a test of maturity sat before me. In a practice done by all treatment clinic programs between the 1960s and mid–1980s. I was given drinking privileges to see if I could drink responsibly.

Chapter 10

Climbing Daytop's Staff Ladder and Leaving

In the summer of 1973, I married Maritza, a woman I met at a disco club and dated for almost a year. She didn't do drugs and would only have an occasional glass of wine.

I worked my way up to Daytop's salaried positions of senior coordinator and then assistant director, with the objective of becoming a director. Soon I began to buckle under the pressure. Emotional weaknesses still gnawed deep inside me, and since the staff was permitted to drink socially, I found myself craving more and more alcohol.

By the time 1976 came around, there still hadn't been any openings for a director at Daytop, so I started looking at other addiction treatment facilities. I learned of the Élan School, a private, coeducational residential behavior-modification and therapeutic school in Androscoggin County, Maine, and called Joe Ricci, its director, who was a former Daytop resident. He immediately offered me an interview for a director's position in its elite VIP program to work at a facility in Maine. I was thrilled, because Joe said he'd not only triple my Daytop salary and include benefits, but that he'd also pay my wife her current salary until she was able to find a new job. On top of those wonderful incentives and perks was that any member of his staff who had completed its treatment program was permitted to drink socially within moderation, but because I wasn't a part of Élan's program, there would be no waiting period for me. I would immediately have the freedom to consume alcohol.

I told Maritza that Joe was sending his private plane to pick me up and take me to the interview and that she should come with me. Off to Maine we both went in Joe's private jet. Joe met us at the Lewiston airport in his brand-new Jaguar and drove us to his mansion on the twenty-acre property he owned in Falmouth. My interview was conducted there, and he immediately offered me the job. After a private discussion with Maritza, I accepted the position, telling him that we would need a little time to find a place to live.

"No problem," he said. "I'll find you a nice house for rent and pay all your moving costs. After that, you'll pay expenses."

I was so excited to get my director's position. Maritza was not so sure about this move so far away from family, but she supported me anyway. Little did I know this was going to be a bad decision and create many problems to deal with.

Chapter 11

Élan and My Directorship

J oe had used Daytop's nonprofit eighteen- to twenty-four-month program as a foundation and tailored it into a profit-making private program for adolescents called Pinehedge School in Poland Springs, Maine, where he made millions for himself. He had met with psychiatrist Dr. Gerald Davidson, who had been working for a methadone maintenance program in Boston, and together they established Élan One Corporation, which generated many millions of dollars.

When I met with Joe for my interview, he explained that Élan One Corporation had schools for addicted adolescents throughout Maine in three locations: one in Parsons Field (its only lockdown facility), a second in Waterford, and a third in Poland Springs. The available director's position was at the Poland Springs facility.

Over the three sites, the corporation maintained six buildings and a couple of trailers that housed between 175 to 250 private and state-referred residents. Joe preferred private, high-profile clients from VIP families, and the fees these clients paid were extremely high.

He advised VIP parents that if their child ran away or was abducted, a tracking team would be sent anywhere on the globe. He believed that the thick backwoods of the Poland Springs location and Maine's long cold winters were strong deterrents to an escape or kidnapping, but new residents at that site who appeared to be potential runaways would have their shoes taken away and be forced to wear shorts. He also told parents that a child who relapsed after completing the program could return for an extended stay at no charge.

It all sounded good, so I signed a two-year contract as director with Élan at its Poland Springs facility, although during the first three-and-a-half years of my employment with the company I would come to work at each of its six facilities. Although I found it fair that misbehaving residents would lose privileges (television, recreation, visitors, home passes), I found some of the program's methods to be downright abusive. For instance, where at Daytop a man would have his head shaved and be forced to wear childlike clothing to resemble the baby he was acting like, Élan's residents who acted like children were placed in a boxing ring and required to fight with the largest resident and be spanked by another resident. As degrading as it sounds, this technique did seem to work—plus I had no choice but to go along with their program, as I was reaping the benefits. While Daytop was affiliated with Yale University's mental-health department, Élan was a private company. Since it did not receive funding from any state source, it could do what it wanted without worrying about state regulations. Joe was the boss, feared by staff and residents alike.

One of the practices instituted at the Poland Springs facility was targeted toward any new resident who came into the program with a bad attitude or who was in noncompliance with the rules. This person would have to sit before a general meeting in front of anywhere between sixty to almost a hundred residents and be berated by them. Joe himself led these meetings to humiliate, intimidate, and instill fear in all who participated. It worked.

One of the buildings at Parsons Field was a maximum-security residence that housed state referrals of children between thirteen and eighteen years of age who had been serving time for heavy crimes like assault, robbery, rape, and murder. The state considered Élan as these children's last possible chance for rehabilitation—and indeed, some would be helped, with many being transferred to Daytop or other facilities, such as mental hospitals. Sadly, though, most were recycled back into the criminal justice system.

A typical day for residents at Élan started with waking up early in the morning, usually between five and seven o'clock, making beds, and cleaning the dormitory area. Breakfast followed at seven-thirty. Afterwards, residents would be required to attend a one-hour morning meeting to coordinate the day and department responsibilities. Job duties filled the time between nine in the morning and five in the evening, along with any education, seminars, and group meetings, which continued through the night. In most cases, staff saw productive results among the young residents. But there were certainly "those" days.

There was one extremely negative kid from Rhode Island who purposely did whatever he could to oppose Élan's programs and rules. Consequently, all behavior modification techniques were utilized—he was placed in the boxing ring, he was spanked, he was beaten up, and he wore signs advertising his misbehaviors around his neck for everyone to read and make fun of. One day he was placed in the shower under scalding hot water that was immediately turned to cold water and then back to hot water and then back to cold water and so on. Afterward, he was placed outside in the freezing subzero weather to shovel snow, and his clothing stuck to him. A few minutes later, he was called back in and returned to alternating hot and cold showers, after which he was again forced to shovel snow outside. This was repeated several times. He soon went into a catatonic state and was placed in a state mental institution.

There was a nurse at our facility who told any kids who were feeling ill that the only thing wrong with them was negative thinking; with positive thinking, they'd feel better. One poor kid kept complaining of not feeling well. This nurse reprimanded him and said all he had to do was to think positive, and she sent him back to work. The next day came, but not for him. He died during the night of spinal meningitis. Thankfully, this incident forced some, if only slight, improvement of Élan's handling of medical issues.

It still seemed as if every day, we'd learn that Élan was being sued for child abuse. Most lawsuits were either dropped or no fault was found. We came to learn that the children interviewed by the Department of Children and Families were afraid of Élan retaliating in some manner, so the kids said they supported the treatment and were benefitting from what was being done to them. Whenever a suit was dropped, Joe would mockingly parade the findings to Élan's staff, who had at one time been addiction residents and endured similar abuse themselves.

Joe knew the weaknesses and vulnerabilities of every staff member from when they were program participants. If they said or did anything in opposition to what he wanted, he would threaten them with discharge. He certainly knew how to press my buttons. I recall one day during Christmas vacation, when Maritza and I were visiting family in Connecticut to celebrate the holiday, he called and said he was extremely upset with one of his regional directors and wanted to demote him. He needed me back for a directors' group meeting. Before I could come up with an excuse, I was told that his private plane would pick me up and that I'd be flown back to Connecticut that same night. Signed to a contract, earning three times the salary I had earned at Daytop, and appreciating Joe's tolerance when I received my first arrest for driving while intoxicated by only issuing me a warning, I flew back.

One day during my directorship, I witnessed an extremely severe child-abuse incident when two regional directors on the Poland Springs property called and instructed me to meet them in the office so that we could go to one of the other buildings. Apparently, several young residents were acting up and had to be controlled. Never having gone through anything similar, I didn't know what to expect. During our walk to the building, the regional directors referred to the kids as "dirt," bragged about how this sort of behavior wasn't going to be tolerated, and explained that they were going to show me how to control it.

As we entered the building, some of the kids were sitting and others were standing, but they immediately quieted down upon seeing us. The directors randomly grabbed kids by the collar, neck, and shirt and slammed them against the nearest wall. The kids would bounce off the wall and fall over couches and chairs onto the floor. Screaming threats to these youngsters of worse physical treatment, the regional directors instructed staff to carry out additional punishments, such as loss of all privileges and walking around with insulting and degrading signs hanging around their necks.

One girl who was thrown over a couch into the wall was a Puerto Rican teenager I would encounter many years later when I was visiting someone in the mental ward at Bridgeport Hospital. The girl—or should I say woman, because when I saw her that second time she was about thirty-five years old and had kids—had a history of health problems both physical and mental, and she had been kicked out of several institutions, one after the other. When she saw me again, she hugged me and started to cry, telling me of several other experiences she had endured at Élan and thanking me for always treating her with respect.

Then there was Raymond, one of Élan's worst and most abused kids. Raymond was from a very poor family, and his treatment was state-funded. Before being sent to Élan at age fourteen, he bounced from facility to facility because he was aggressive, couldn't get along with others, and was noncompliant with rules. By the time I arrived at Élan, he had been there for three or four years. Raymond was always being put into the boxing ring, and never once did he defend himself or fight back. He stoically took every beating until he would simply break down and cry. It was so sad. No one liked him. I tried to guide him as kindly as possible, and he was usually fine with me, but as soon as he was with someone else, he'd return to his hostile disposition. They discharged him when he was twenty-one, and I never learned what became of him.

There were also kids in the program who were cutters, meaning that they would mutilate themselves. They were always accompanied by another resident and given boxing gloves to wear most of the time so they couldn't cut themselves. Since they received very little counseling, if any, this was the only method used until everyone felt assured they wouldn't cut anymore.

It is with deep, deep sorrow that I acknowledge there were many, many stories similar to the few I've written about here.

Chapter 12

The Rich and Famous Residents

The wealthier kids at Élan were the children, grandchildren, nieces, and nephews of movie stars, rock stars, CEOs of large companies, lawyers, and so on. One youngster named Ed was from an enormously wealthy VIP family. He always wore clothing that advertised where he was from—cowboy hat and boots, studded vest, shirt, jeans, and a tie. He walked around with a very haughty attitude, acting as if he was better than everyone else because of his family's high-society profile. His attitude didn't sit very well with Joe, and even though the kid hadn't done anything wrong, he was called before a general meeting of close to a hundred staff and residents from all three buildings at Poland Springs so that he could be belittled and demoralized.

During the meeting, Joe sarcastically described Ed's upscale background, and then everyone chimed in, yelling and mockingly berating the poor kid. It wasn't long before Joe threw Ed's cowboy hat on the floor and jumped on top of it until it was completely flattened out, and then he angrily ripped Ed's vest apart. Then, making Ed remove his boots, Joe wildly banged them on the floor. Afterward, Joe sent the boy into the boxing ring, where he was outfitted with headgear, gloves, and a mouthpiece. An extremely large fellow resident with boxing experience climbed into the ring and proceeded to beat Ed badly.

Led to lean over a chair afterward, Ed was spanked by his peers, who screamed at him that his behavior had to change. Ed was then assigned a big brother who stayed with him every day, every hour, and every minute to monitor his attitude and continue chastising him. Finally realizing and accepting that he was outnumbered, Ed conformed to the facility's demands.

One resident staff member with whom I became friendly was a graduate of the program. Allen was the brother of musician Glenn Frey—singer, songwriter, guitarist, and pianist with the popular rock band the Eagles, who recently died at age sixty-seven because of medical complications. Shortly before I arrived at Élan, Allen had arranged for the band to play at the facility. To this day, I'm disappointed I wasn't around at the time.

Then there was the time, while I was director, when Linda Ronstadt's nephew was a resident. Whenever her nephew acted inappropriately, I would call her for permission to place him in the boxing ring. She was a very down-to-earth person and easy to talk to. During our first conversation, Linda told me of the fortune she had spent trying to help him get off drugs. She also talked about the money she spent on his dental work and asked that I make sure he wore headgear and a mouthpiece the entire time. She'd say, "Just don't kill the mother."

ASSOCIATED PRESS FILE PHOTO

Forty years ago today, the Greenwich community was stunned by a savage crime committed on that date.

Martha Moxley, a popular 15-year-old Greenwich High School sophomore, was murdered, bludgeoned by a golf club and stabbed in the neck with its broken shaft. The murder weapon, a ladies 6-iron, was traced to the Skakel property across the street from Moxley's home in the exclusive Belle Haven section of town.

Also in residence during my time at Élan was the infamous accused murderer Michael Skakel, a Kennedy relative. On the very cold wintry day of March 10, 1978, I received a call from Joe saying that the chief executive officer wanted to speak with me. When I arrived at his office, Joe and Dr. Davidson were sitting there. I was told that a VIP was going to be placed in my facility and I would be working with this individual. I was then informed that the person was Ethel Kennedy's nephew Michael Skakel.

They asked if I knew about the 1975 murder in Greenwich, Connecticut, of a young girl named Martha Moxley, which Mr. Skakel had been accused of committing. I said that being from Connecticut, I had heard about it, but I wasn't aware of the specifics. I was then told a few details about the murder and that the Skakel brothers were suspects. I was also told that during the time Michael Skakel would be at Élan, he was prevented from talking about the case and could only speak about it privately with Dr. Davidson.

Michael was known for having difficulties with accepting reality, growing up, and taking responsibility. He acted as if rules didn't apply to him. When reprimanded, he would immaturely laugh. The one thing Michael could not avoid was that every time he was in any type of group setting with his peers who also were

VIP residents, they would bring up the murder and consistently confront him about why he murdered Martha Moxley. Although I would intervene and try to stop him from responding, Michael nonetheless would say how fucked up it was, shuffle in his chair, run his hands through his hair, and then crouch over, holding onto his stomach as he cried. Other times, he'd simply run out of the room, which us staffers knew was a sure sign of substance-abuse behavior. Ultimately, though, he saw that the group members genuinely cared about him. With time, he opened up more and talked about his true feelings.

Everyone at the facility became aware that Michael would share his thoughts and feelings about the murder with peers outside of the therapeutic groups he attended, such as at recreation, during smoke breaks, on the back porch, or in his dorm. One day, we learned that Michael had admitted to another resident that he did murder the girl, but that he was going to get away with it because he was a Kennedy. When Joe heard about this, he called for a three-house general meeting which the staff, Michael, and his peers attended.

What Michael had said and his actions were openly discussed. It was agreed that in order to help him address his feelings associated with the murder, he should carry a sign around his neck that read,

"Ask me why I killed my friend, Martha Moxley." It was believed that because the subject was now available for open discussion with anyone at the facility, Michael would have to start truthfully facing himself.

Many years later, when I was working in Connecticut with the Department of Corrections and interviewing an inmate for possible placement into the community APT Foundation's release program (a substance-abuse program I'll discuss later in the book), I came across Michael in the visitor's room during the time he was awaiting trial. At my greeting, he first had a puzzled look, but after a few moments he smiled and said hello. Michael received a sentence of twenty years to life. In 2014, after spending twelve years in Connecticut's state prison, he was released on an appeal bond on the grounds that his attorney misrepresented him, and the matter is still pending before the court at the time of this writing. Had Michael pled guilty to Martha Moxley's murder when he was fifteen years old, he might have spent just six years in a juvenile detention home rather than twelve years in Connecticut's state prison with the possibility of additional imprisonment.

Michael's situation brings another case to mind. At the Connecticut Department of Corrections, where I worked for over thirty-eight years after leaving Élan, I met a man who received a life sentence for murdering his mother-in-law with a bowling pin. He only served nine years and eventually became the warden of the New Haven Correctional Center. It was alcohol that ultimately led to his downfall. He was fired and had to deal with his alcohol problem. I hope he has done well.

Chapter 13

Leaving Élan

In December of 1978, while driving in Maine on a work-related errand, I was in a very serious car accident (ironically, the truck that hit my car had many empty beer cans in its cab). I was unconscious, and then suddenly I came to, jolted awake by a bright white light, brighter than the sun. An old man with whiskers and just a few teeth, who looked like a bum, knocked on my window and yelled, "Get out of the car! It's on fire!"

Just then, the EMTs arrived. They carried me to the side of the road and laid me down. I was gasping for air and in severe pain … and then the car exploded. I looked around for the man who had alerted me to get out of the car, but he was nowhere to be found. I asked the EMT staff where he went, and they replied that there was no one near the car when they pulled me out. It was another miracle from God in my life.

I was severely injured. Unaware that Maritza and I had recently separated because of my alcoholism, the hospital called her and my older sister, Alice, telling them I was in critical condition and not expected to live and that they should come quickly to say their good-byes.

I spent thirty-nine days in the hospital on a strict liquid diet. My spleen was removed. My pancreas was so damaged that a drain was attached to it for over a year. I went from 180 pounds to 110 pounds. One day, Maritza told me she was pregnant with our first child (which would be our only child), but because of my expected demise, reconciliation wasn't even broached.

On the fortieth day, the hospital called Alice and said it was best that I be discharged so that I would be surrounded by family and friends when I died, an outcome that was highly expected. My cat Frisco and I went to live with my sister Carol in Connecticut. Amazingly and wonderfully, three or four months later I was back on my feet, and Maritza and I decided to give our marriage another try for the sake of our unborn child. I also went back to work at Élan.

One evening during the first week of August 1979, Joe's wife (who was an inspiration for Joe's successes) and I were planning a baby shower for Maritza. We went to a local bar to discuss the upcoming event. Because I had a personal history of three violations for driving under the influence, we went in her car, but when we left I strongly suggested that I drive, because it was just too enticing for me to drive her Mercedes. Moments later, the revolving lights of a police car showed in the rearview mirror. I was given a summons to appear in court, where I received a large fine and my driver's license suspension was extended. And Joe terminated me.

My wife and I remained in Maine until our daughter was born at the end of August, 1979. During this time, I telephoned my friend Vinny Nuzzo, who was the director at Daytop at the time. He immediately suggested I return to college, because recovering addicts could no longer be hired as directors. He also arranged an interview for me through Vincent Brescia, CEO of the Center for Human Services regional network of programs in Bridgeport, Connecticut.

I flew to Boston, interviewed, and was hired for a managerial position starting in late October at one of Bridgeport's halfway homes, overseeing ten federal parolees and ten state parolees. During the second week of October, Maritza, our daughter, our pet cat, and I moved back to Connecticut.

Joe went on to become a multimultimillionaire by buying the Scarborough Downs racetrack and Cumberland County racetrack, plus many acres of property in Portland, Maine. He also ran for governor of Maine twice, but lost both times.

Chapter 14

A College Degree, New Jobs ... and Still Drinking

We settled in Fairfield, Connecticut, the town next to the one where Maritza's family lived in Bridgeport. I immediately started working and signed up for college courses held on weekends which were geared toward the working person. All this time, I was still a functioning alcoholic.

In February of 1981, I was promoted to director of Bridgeport's methadone maintenance program, replacing the prior director who had left under suspicion of selling methadone on the street. Because many of the employees were not doing their jobs, I immediately fired four. Later that month, the remaining employees, upset that I had fired several of their cronies, conspired to have me fired. And so, I was soon terminated.

Day after day, I submitted my résumé to human-services-related organizations, to no avail. Maritza got a job and I stayed home with our daughter for the next year, delightedly potty-training her, teaching her to walk, and more. I earned my bachelor of sciences degree in human services and, shortly after my graduation in May 1981, when our daughter was exactly twenty-two months old, I was hired as a vocational instructor at a school for autistic, multi-handicapped teenagers who needed to learn basic living skills to function in society as adults. Because quite a lot of them had been institutionalized for most if not all of their lives, the job was depressing and I was only able to remain there for a year.

I contacted someone I knew well who was the chief executive officer of the Connecticut Renaissance drug program, and in mid-1982, I was hired as director of the residential program. I was still drinking and was often late to work. I missed several days and easily lost my temper. Although reprimanded, I couldn't act any differently. Consequently, in October of 1983, I lost my job. At that point, my alcohol consumption became almost uncontrollable.

Right before the Christmas holiday, I had an acute pancreatic attack and was rushed to the hospital next door to where I was living. The attack soon subsided, but not before the doctor told me that I could not drink any more alcohol ever, as alcohol was the cause of my condition. He planned on discharging me the following day. Without explanation, he added that he wanted me to speak with someone first.

A short while later, an African-American man came into my room, sat in the chair next to my bed, and began to tell me his life story. Needless to say, I was a captive audience. He told me he was addicted to alcohol and that he had a medical condition similar to mine. He told me that he knew of a way to stop drinking. I immediately became defensive, stating that perhaps it was good for him, but I didn't have a drinking problem. He continued to speak about a fellowship of men and women who, together, learned how to stop drinking by helping each other. I thanked him for the information, and he left the room.

With Christmas and the New Year around the corner, all I could think of was getting home so that I could celebrate with a drink. That's just what I did. The problem was, I could never stop at just one drink. On February 1, I again found myself in enormous pain, and I knew it was another acute pancreatic attack. I asked Maritza to take me to the hospital, but she was completely fed up with my drinking at this point and told me to get to the hospital myself. So that's what I did.

In my hospital room, the doctor told me she had lost trust in me and that she was going to find a bed for me at a detox rehabilitation center. She also said Maritza told her I wasn't welcome back home. I got nervous about where I'd go and if I still had a marriage left. Bill, the man who had told me about his drinking problem the last time I was hospitalized, came to mind; but I still denied having an uncontrollable addiction to alcohol. After all, I'd been able to stop heroin and hard drugs when I wanted to.

When I recovered from this pancreatic attack, both Maritza and the doctor told me they had reserved a bed for me in a detox facility. In early February 1984, I was taken to Hall Brooke Behavioral Health Services in Westport, Connecticut, wondering what I was doing in a mental hospital. Little did I know that this would become the beginning of my second life.

Chapter 15

My Second Life Begins

Upon admittance to the rehab center, I was surprised to see Flo, a woman I had hired in 1980 at the halfway house as a night counselor. She asked if I was applying for a job there. I was mortified with embarrassment. Here I was, a former director of several drug rehabilitation programs, a man who had been free of illegal drug consumption for twelve years, being admitted for treatment. She wished me well, and I was placed in a twenty-eight-day detox program.

The first few days of going through withdrawal were difficult, even though the staff was kind and truly concerned with how I was coming along. I attended group sessions and fellowship meetings where everyone would openly speak about the problems that prompted their addiction. I finally realized that I was identifying with some of these people.

The more I attended these meetings, the more clearly I saw the truth that I did, indeed, have an uncontrollable drinking problem. Bill's story about his alcohol addiction kept resonating in my head, and so I accepted that I was part of an alcohol-addiction-recovery fellowship group. I began making friends with the members. Even after being discharged from the detox program, I continued to go to these meetings.

I graduated Hall Brooke's detox program in March of 1984. This was to be my last detox and my last drink of alcohol. To this day, I am going on thirty-three years clean and sober. But I remained unemployed, and by the time January of 1985 rolled around, I was desperate enough to contact Daytop, although I felt a little weird because I had quit in 1976. I decided to give it a shot anyway and contacted Vinny Nuzzo, who was still a director there.

Vinny told me that for financial reasons, Daytop had merged with APT Foundation, another addiction treatment organization, although it was still operating under the name of Daytop. He said a job opening was coming up in a few weeks at the Newtown, Connecticut, facility. I became disheartened when I learned that I would have to start at the bottom again as a counselor and work up to a director's position. My ego had difficulty accepting that, but at least I would be able to return. So up the salaried clinical-professional ladder I went, from counselor I to counselor II to senior counselor and then to assistant director.

Also permitted to become part of Daytop's clinical professional staff were residents who had graduated its treatment program, but it hadn't always been that way. When Daytop first started, a recovered addict could work as a staff member after graduating the program and receiving certification by the state of Connecticut. The "clinical professionals" working at Daytop, however, were outside specialists who hadn't gone through the program. Daytop's new system allowed for recovered staff to work in a professional capacity as well, and both designations become equal.

At the end of 1985, Daytop's program changed. Its old therapeutic concept of addiction based on dysfunction, discomfort, or distress rarely worked anymore, so a new medical model was put into effect that established addiction as a disease with biological, neurological, genetic, and environmental sources of origin. Sometime around 1994, Vinny Nuzzo was asked to resign. He had reverted back to the therapeutic concept and made a resident wear a derogatory sign around his neck.

The end of 1985 was also around the time the facility stopped operating under the name of Daytop and was renamed APT

Residential Services. I still wonder why that specific location in Bridgeport was renamed, since Daytop was still going strong in New York and in forty-eight countries around the world. Regardless, I thank Daytop from the bottom of my heart for all it did for me in helping me start my second life.

In early 2000, in addition to being an APT assistant director, I served as court liaison/criminal-justice liaison with the prison community release program. I'd go to various prisons, courts, and probation departments to interview clients for APT's short-term and residential long-term treatment programs. Even though the name of the Bridgeport facility changed from Daytop to APT in 1980 when they merged, out of habit I continued to use the Daytop name with prisoners as well as with APT's residents.

One day, I was called to the APT office and prohibited from repeating the name anymore to anyone anywhere. My instincts told me I had been targeted for termination and that my days at the facility were numbered. (Ironically, from 2006 to 2009, APT still used Daytop's name to apply for funding from the Department of Corrections, stating that the funds related to referrals within the surrounding communities. Ultimately, though, when patrons would not stay for the full program and attendees became fewer and fewer, the truth came to light and less and less funding was provided.)

To ensure I'd have an income if I was terminated, I decided to start a part-time business while I was still working at APT. I started a limousine driving service; I would drive passengers to and from the airport before work, after work, and on weekends while still interviewing prospective APT residents to fill the twenty-eight to thirty beds I was responsible for overseeing. Even though I continued for years to feel insecure about my job, I was still working at APT in December of 2008 when I had a bad slip and fall in the facility's parking lot. I tore my quadricep, which dislocated my hip, and I filed a workers' compensation claim. I had to wear a brace twenty-four hours a day for eight weeks and went through rehabilitation for nine months. During this entire time, I walked with a cane. In September of 2009, I went on medical leave to have my right hip replaced.

The personnel policy at APT allowed up to six months of medical leave with pay. Unlike a coworker who went through alcohol rehabilitation for one week but stayed out for almost six weeks on a binge drunk and got paid for the entire time out, I returned to work on November 6, 2009, a little less than two months after the operation. Three weeks later, I was called to human resources and told I was being laid off because someone at APT's access center in New Haven would be handling the responsibilities of my job with criminal justice. My last day of employment would be one week before Christmas, on December 18, 2009.

I was sixty-four at the time. Although I had been expecting to be terminated since the debacle over my mentioning Daytop to prisoners and in therapy sessions, I was still shocked. That astonishment deepened when I received absolutely no severance pay whatsoever after a total of thirty-eight years of service working for Daytop and APT. I was thankful, though, that I'd had the foresight to start my driving service.

I remained in touch with the fellowship of rehabilitated men and women addicts and also opened another part-time business performing crisis intervention management. Through word of mouth, I would be referred to people who needed addiction recovery and rehabilitation assistance. I met with addicts at their home, in jail, wherever I was needed.

Not long after I left APT, I learned from a friend that my job had actually been given to a younger person for less money. I discussed this with an attorney pal of mine who convinced me to sue for wrongful termination and age discrimination. We deservedly won the case.

Chapter 16

Some Fun Memories

While at Daytop during the year 2000, I attended a couple of memorable events regarding addiction treatment. One was a dinner party at the World Federation of Therapeutic Communities in San Francisco, California. Attendees representing hope and recovery services from countries all around the globe participated. The mayor at that time was Willie Brown, and he hosted this event at the governor's mansion. Prior to the dinner, a bay cruise to view the city was provided to those who were interested.

This event is where I first met Daytop's founder, Monsignor William B. O'Brien, and its executive officers, Charles J. Devlin, George DeLeon, PhD, and David A. Deitch, PhD (who, along with Ron Broncato, were the first directors of Daytop Village and former members of the drug rehab facility Synanon in Santa Monica,

California). The conference had representatives from all forty-eight countries in which Daytop had facilities.

I also met actor Robert Downey Jr., who was recovering from this disease of addiction. I was friends with his uncle, Jim Downey of Westport, Connecticut, who would often talk to me about how we could help his nephew. At this party, Robert Downey Jr. brought up nearby Walden House and its concept, which was similar to the Daytop program; it too had a well-balanced program with a staff of recovered addicts. Also at the party was Danny Glover, who was a volunteer at Walden House. His brother, Reggie, had been a counselor there after graduating the treatment program in 1993.

The other event was the 5K run "for a drug-free world" in which I participated as a runner. The director at that time, Alfonso P. Acampora, organized this run, which occurred simultaneously around the world. Gaudenzia Drug and Alcohol Rehab, located in San Francisco, California, was established in 1968 by Daytop staff from New York.

Chapter 17

On My Own

The real estate crash of 2008 came down hard on me, and I lost three-quarters of my pension with the Teachers Insurance and Annuity Association—College Retirement Equities Fund (TIAA-CREF). Still residing in Connecticut, I found the cost of living to be so far over my head that I would need to work a third job in order to comfortably afford expenses. So, after receipt of the settlement from the APT lawsuit and seeing the affordable housing market in Florida, I sold whatever I didn't think I truly needed, packed the rest up, and moved to southern Florida.

My wife at the time, Pamela, and I were splitting up; she wanted to be in New York, and I wanted to retire to Florida. We are still great friends, and the same is true with Maritza, the mother of my daughter, Uriela. Uriela is married and doing well. She never had a substance abuse problem and is a fine responsible women. I'm semiretired and still involved in helping people learn how to help themselves. I'm a certified addiction professional in the state of Florida, as well as a criminal justice/court liaison, crisis intervention manager, and motivational speaker.

Truthfully, the last thirty-two years of my life—my second life— have been the best. In this, my story of recovery and redemption, you will recall my unhappiness in my first life, where I spent way too many years in institutions because of my addictions. The person I was at that time is barely recognizable in my thoughts and memories. I don't feel I resemble him anymore.

My incarcerations have been formally pardoned by the government. In learning about addiction recovery groups all over the world, I have found a wonderful local fellowship of men and women. If you find yourself looking for a way out of a life packed with drugs and/or alcohol and negativity, rest assured, there's a way out, no matter how far you have fallen. Seek the fellowship of men and women who will show you the way. God bless you.

The End

About the Author

I was born in Hartford Connecticut. I grew up in the projects that were infested with negativity, drugs and violence. My first life was full of the above after spending 10 years of my life in jails, prisons and rehabilitation centers. Until I found out a way to get out of all this insanity.

My second life started in 1971 when I entered the Daytop program is Seymore Connecticut . Going from jail to Daytop then to Yale where I worked for over 30 years for one of their affiliates in Connecticut. Since then I completed high school, receive a four-year college degree at the new Hampshire College in New Hampshire in bachelor of science and human services.going from jail to Daytop then to Yale, where I worked for over 30 years for one of their affiliates. My many positions held and achievements include assistant director of the Daytop Apt Foundation, criminal justice court liaison and Department of correction private contractor for community release programs , NA/AA consultant. Resident director of Connecticut renaissance a drug and alcohol rehab. Center. Also Bridgeport methodone maintenance program as their director. Danberry federal prison drug rehabilitation project consultant. Proffessional development. In 1997 I was educational speaker for the narcotic enforcement officers conference for the north east chapter. Therapeutic community training and technical assistance for Ohio department of alcohol and drug addiction (ODADAS), as clinical consultant. Therapeutic community training for the Louisiana Department of public services and safety corrections as clinical consultant. Presently I hold a C.A.P. Certification as a certified addiction professional here in Florida/crisis intervention management and court/criminal justice liaison . I am also a motivational speaker.